1 MONTH OF
FREE
READING

at
www.ForgottenBooks.com

By purchasing this book you are eligible for one month membership to ForgottenBooks.com, giving you unlimited access to our entire collection of over 1,000,000 titles via our web site and mobile apps.

To claim your free month visit:

www.forgottenbooks.com/free920534

ISBN 978-0-266-99449-7
PIBN 10920534

Third Annual Announcement

and Catalogue

Copiah-Lincoln
Agricultural High School

1917-1918
WESSON, MISSISSIPPI

1917
The Lincoln County Times
aven, Miss.

BOARD OF TRUSTEES.

OFFICIAL EDUCATIONAL DIRECTORY.

BOARDS OF EDUCATION.

Copiah County.
A. S. Thomas_____Crystal Springs
L. M. Little_____Rockport
W. W. Furr_____Allen, Miss.
J. A. Stafley_____Carpenter
J. P. Clower_____Crystal Springs

Lincoln County.
John May_____Brookhaven, R. 2
B. E. Summers_____Brookhaven, R. 1
Ira Beeson_____Monticello, R. 1
Walter Denman_____Auburn
Ben P. Smith_____Brookhaven, R. 6

BOARDS OF SUPERVISORS.

Lincoln County.
S. P. Oliver_____Brookhaven
C. M. Brister_____Bogue Chitto
Willie Furr_____Wesson, R. F. D.
C. C. Coleman_____Brookhaven, R. No. 3
J. E. Moak_____Bogue Chitto

Copiah County.
George B. Nelson_____Hazlehurst
S. F. Lusk_____Beauregard
M. E. Furr_____Allen
W. E. Purser_____Carpenter
C. G. Erwin_____Crystal Springs

Mrs. Myrtle S. Dodds, County Home Demonstra-
tion Agent_____Hazlehurst
John C. Anderson, County Agent_____Hazlehurst, Miss.

FACULTY.

R. L. LANDIS
Superintendent.
Education, Psychology

HENRY BARRON
Assistant Superintendent.
Mathematics, History, Civics.

W. H. ALDERMAN
Agriculturalist.
Agriculture, Animal Husbandry, Manual Arts.

MISS GERTRUDE DAVIS
English, Latin, Spanish.

MISS ELMA JONES
Domestic Arts, First Year.

MISS MATTIE FURR
Orthography, Matron.

MISS MILDRED KEITHLEY
Piano, Voice, Expression.

DR. W. L. LITTLE
School Physician, Director of Sanitation.

CALENDAR.

Special.

August 13, 1917, Monday, 9:00 A. M.—Boys' Special Summer School.

August 18, 1917, Saturday—Boys' Summer School Closes.

First Semester.

September 3, 1917, 10:30 A. M.—Faculty Meeting.

September 3, 1917, 1:30 P. M.—Matriculation, Registration, Opening Dormitories, Assignment of Rooms in Dormitories.

September 4, 1917, 10:00 A. M.—Opening Exercises.

November 29, 1917—Thanksgiving Holiday.

December 21, 1917—Christmas Holidays Begin.

December 31, 1917—Christmas Holidays Close.

January 11 and 12, 1918—First Examination.

Second Semester.

January 13, 1918—Second Semester Begins.

May 12, 1918, 11 A. M.—Commencement Sermon.

May 14 and 15, 1918—Final Examinations.

May 16, 1918—Commencement Exercises.

May 17, 1918—Adjournment.

Copiah-Lincoln Agricultural High School.

GREETING.

There has perhaps never been a time in all our country's history when we stood so much in need of trained citizenship as now and as we press through the world crisis we shall find the world more and more in need of trained hands, trained minds and trained hearts. The day is now upon us when we must PREPARE FOR THE GREATEST SERVICE that it may be within our ability to render. The day is upon us, when it is no less than CRIMINAL TO FAIL TO PREPARE for meeting life's duties with true Education. True Education is nothing short of a full development of human faculties. An education that fails to develop the head, the heart and the hand is only a partial education and fails to develop the full, well rounded life. No one capable of good reasoning thinks of omitting the intellectual training. Only those, and we believe they are few, who are immoral would think of tolerating a neglect of the moral development of a child. In this period of world necessity and world demand can it be less than criminal to a young man or a young woman to fail to develop the hand? Can it be less, with the present demands of society than an injustice to society to fail to give by some means vocational training to all our young people that they may be able to do the best service to themselves and others?

There are no institutions within the bounds of our country we believe for the training in all phases of education so broad as the Agricultural High Schools. There is no other sort of high school in the State that offers so

broad and well filled curriculum as the Agricultural High
School. A literary course of study broader than the average high school, with advantages of agricultural training, manual arts and Domestic Arts gives them an ad-
vantage that at present is impossible for other schools.

As a proof of the correct idea of the Agricultural
High School is the tendency of schools of the literary type
to attempt the teaching in manual and domestic arts, the
fostering of Club Work.

Agricultural Schools throughout the State stand for
the dignity of honest toil especially that which dignifies
rural home making and home keeping and these phases
of educational work and school life for boys and girls are
the **leading parts** of the Curriculum of the **Copiah-Lincoln Agricultural High School.**

We are not striving to prepare boys and girls for
college in a literary way and dismiss them, often without means to go to college upon but to enable them to
grapple with the problems of life as they exist in our own
counties, or enter any college or university with superior
advantages.

It is desired that the school be the educational cen-
tre of the community. Citizens of the counties and of
the State are invited to call upon the school for any assistance pertaining to school, farm or home life, that it
may be possible for the school to render.

DESCRIPTION.

The school has two large dormitories, one for boys,
one for girls. Meals are served from the same dining
hall. Each dormitory is amply provided with good substantial furniture. Each has been planned after general convenience and economy. In each building is found
a drinking fountain, bath-rooms, and general sanitary
arrangements.

The Administration building is one of the most mod
ern and conveniently arranged in the country well ligh-

ted, well ventilated, provided with telephone and other conveniences.

LOCATION.

New Orleans is one hundred and thirty miles south, Jackson about forty five miles north. A gravel pike runs through the farm, and extends more than a hundred miles north passing through Hazlehurst, Gallman, Crystal Springs, Jackson and other points of importance. With improved roads to the south, Brookhaven, Bogue Chitto, McComb and other points are easily reached.

The pike mentioned is a part of the proposed Jefferson Davis Highway.

The healthfulness of the location is all that can be desired, the elevation is good, drainage almost perfect.

GENERAL INFORMATION.

The school shall strive to ever hold before the student body a high ideal of life, to ever emphasize the dignity of honest toil.

The life of any boarding school should furnish the student with better ideas and better realization of what it means to be truly educated from a sense of moral, cultural, and social development. The text books do not and cannot form more than a small percent of the fundamentals of true education.

Education from the origin of the word shows that it means development.

Development of human life cannot fail to mean if given its full significance the development of the threefold nature of man, the physical, the intellectual, the moral or spiritual. Any system of education that neglects either phase is at least incomplete.

The school shall at all times be glad to give any assistance possible to school communities in solution of school or educational problems, to render any aid to

dairymen or dairy farmers, general farmers or those in-
terested in live stock.

Come and visit classes when in session and see what
we are doing.

We want your boys and girls if prepared to enter
high school or take academic work provided they are
of good habits and come for business, but we are not
not running a reformatory and do not desire any that are
incorrigible. **We do not care for any student not will-
ing to be corrected.**

Apply early for rooms, we reserve the right to as-
sign rooms and do not extend pupils privilege of select-
ing rooms or to change rooms **except on written consent of
the Superintendent.**

EXPENSES.

No tuition charged to students from Copiah or Lincoln counties.

Pupils from other counties shall be charged $2.00
per month, one half of which shall be paid in advance
and the remainder at close of the fourth scholastic month.

Non-resident students shall not receive a refund on
tuition on leaving school before expiration of term.

A matriculation fee of $3.00 shall be charged all
students boarding in dormitory on entering school; all
others shall pay $1.50.

The matriculation fee shall be used for general in-
cidental expenses.

In addition to the matriculation fee Dormitory students shall pay a medical fee of $3.00 per year, one dol-
lar of which shall be paid at opening of school and one
dollar at close of third month and one dollar at close
of sixth month.

The fee thus collected shall provide drugs not requiring a prescription, sanitary attention of premises, and
instruction and attention of physician, care for the sick
for a period of time not to exceed one week if necessary.

This shall not be construed to mean that patent medicines may be secured or chronic troubles treated. A physician other than the school physician must be at the student's expense.

Board in the dormitory shall be given at actual cost, which shall be made as low as possible in order to be amply provided.

To save enquiries we wish to state that we have no work to offer or any means to give students to pay board, tuition, matriculation or medical fees.

Board must be paid one month in advance. If any delay is made in payment the rate of board shall be subject to an increase of fifteen cents per day for each day's delay and **ten days delay shall subject a pupil to suspension.**

Money paid in advance for board shall be refunded by the estimate of the Superintendent if compelled to discontinue school because of providential reasons.

No deduction shall be made for loss of time for any thing less than one half month except on entrance.

For the first month students must deposit $7.50 for board, this with matriculation and medical fee makes necessary for entrance $11.50. Notice we have not increased cost by occasion of high prices.

Our expenses for the first two years is shown by these figures: 1915-1916—Matriculation fee $3.00 (used for incidental expenses and general good of school); Medical fee $3.00, (Physician and medicine when needed); total board 9 months $49.79; average cost board $5.53 per school month; average cost all expenses $6.19 2-3 plus.

1916-1917—Matriculation $3.00; Medical $3.00; total board $54.33; average board $6.03 2-3; average cost all expenses $6.70 1-3 plus.

Our students are well provided for as most of them will testify. They almost invariably gain in weight on coming into dormitory and as a rule do better work than those living or boarding elsewhere.

We promise to make next year's expenses as low as possible to be amply provided for and if we get good crops do not dread the high prices that prevail. We have now as property of Boarding Department a number of good hogs that we are growing at a minimum expense which will largely provide meat for next year if we carry out our plans.

Often we can buy from the student or patron, produce, canned goods, and meat. We are trying to raise all potatoes and corn necessary.

ENTRANCE REQUIREMENTS.

1. All pupils must have completed the eighth grade work in public schools before entering Copiah-Lincoln Agricultural High School.

2. Any student expecting to enter any grade should bring a report from last school attended or a certificate from last teacher certifying work completed and grade made in order that an entrance examination may not be necessary.

3. **A written certificate of good character shall be required** from all those not personally known to the Superintendent from some teacher, minister, banker, business man, or person of unquestioned character.

4. Each student shall on entering school be required to sign the following pledge: "I DO PROMISE UPON MY HONOR THAT WHILE A STUDENT OF THE CO-PIAH-LINCOLN AGRICULTURAL HIGH SCHOOL NOT TO HAVE IN MY POSSESSION ANY TOBACCO OR TO USE IT IN ANY FORM, OR ANY KIND OF FIRE ARMS OR GAMBLING APPARATUS, NOT TO DRINK OR BRING ON THE CAMPUS, OR IN THE SCHOOL OR DORMITORY, ANY FORM OF AN INTOXICANT AND NOT TO LEAVE SCHOOL LIMITS WITHOUT PERMISSION FROM PROPER AUTHORITY." (Pen-

alty for any of these offenses to be accepted from Super-intendent, or Superintendent and faculty as final).

COURSE OF STUDY.

First Year—B Section.

Agriculture—Water's Essentials.
Domestic Art—Principles and Applications (Bailey).
English—Kern and Noble's First Book.
> Classics—Christmas Carol, Dickens; Rime of Ancient Mariner; The Autobiography, Franklin, Julius Cæsar, Shakespeare.
> Supplemental—as may be selected.
Orthography—Assigned by teacher.
Arithmetic—Colaw and Elwood, Advanced.
Algebra—Milne's Standard.
Latin—Beginning Smith's Latin Lessons.
Drill Work—Direction of teacher.

First Year—A Section.

Agriculture—Water's Essentials.
Domestic Art—Principles and Applications.
Orthography—Assigned by teacher.
English—Advanced Grammar (to be selected).
Classics—As in B Section.
Arithmetic—Colaw & Elwood, Advanced completed.
Algebra—Milne's Standard.
Drill Work—Direction of Faculty.
Elective—
> General Science—Clark.
> Latin—Construction, Fables Extracts from Cæsar.
> Drill Work—Composition.

Second Year.

Agriculture: Boys—Southern Field Crops (Duggar).
Domestic Art: Girls—Bailey.
English: Composition—Brook's.

English: Classics—Vicar of Wakefield, Goldsmith; Bryant's Poems; Selection from Tennyson.
Algebra—Milne's Standard, completed.
History—West's Ancient World, with Crown Series Historical Outlines.
Orthography—Assigned by teacher.
Drill Work—Assigned by teacher.
Elective—
    Latin—Cæsar (Walker).
    Physiography.—.

Junior Year.

Agriculture: Boys—Harper's Animal Husbandry.
Domestic Art: Girls.
Orthography—Chew's Speller.
English Literature—Halleck.
English: Supplemental—Baskerville and Sewall's Grammar.
English: Classics—Macbeth; Milton's Short Poems; Silas Marner.
Drill Work—Direction of Faculty.
History—Modern World (West).
Geometry, Plane—Wentworth and Smith.
Elective (select two)—
    Physics—Gorton's High School.
    Latin—Cicero (Walker).
    German or Spanish.
    Book-keeping.

Senior Year.

Agriculture: Boys—Farm Management. (Warren); Machinery and Surveying (to be selected).
Domestic Art: Girls—Bulletins, Tried Experiments.
Geometry: Solid—Wentworth and Smith.
Algebra—
History—United States (Cousin and Hill) with Crown Series Historical Outlines.

Civics—Government in The United States (Garner).
History of Education—Graver.
English—History of American Literature (Halleck).
English: Classics—Hamlet; Emerson's Essays; Study of
      Current Events Based on Independent Maga-
      zine and other leading periodicals.
Orthography and Drill Work—Direction of Faculty.
Elective Subjects (Elect two)—
    Latin—Virgil.
    Spanish.
    Pedagogy.
    Psychology.
    Book-keeping.

GRADUATION.

A minimum of twenty two units shall be required for graduation. At least two of these units must be for practical work. These cannot be granted for work with an average of less than a grade of 80 per centum.

DOMESTIC ARTS.

Miss Elma Jones, Instructor.

It is aimed that this department give a practical, scientific knowledge of goods, clothing, practical housekeeping and sanitation, and it will be the purpose to make each lesson a step for useful living. Economy will be the study; true beauty in the home, the idea which will be developed.

Preparatory Year.

ELEMENTARY COOKERY.—This includes the fundamental principles of practical cooking, emphasis being laid on accuracy, neatness, and economy. The aim of this course will be to train each student to be capable of cooking and serving the average family meal. Three times a week, double periods.

SEWING.—This includes practice in common practical stitches and the application of these to garments.

First Year.

ELEMENTARY COOKERY.—This includes practice in bread-making, cake-making and desserts. Menus will be planned according to balanced rations, prepared and served.

Second Year.

ADVANCED COOKERY.—Nutrition and diet will be studied; invalid foods prepared and served. Emphasis will be laid on canning and preserving.

SEWING.—A continuation of work begun in First year.

Third Year.

HOUSES DECORATION.—A study of floors, wall paper, kitchens, dining rooms, bed rooms, living rooms, and bath rooms.

Emphasis will be laid on suitability of furnishings.

SEWING.—A continuation of work of second year. Required that each student graduate in simple clothing made in the department.

SPECIAL DEPARTMENT.

Miss Mildred Keithley, Director.

Work in Piano, Voice, and Expression under supervision of Miss Keithley who enters upon her work with enthusiasm.

We believe this class shall do splendid work and hope from the class much help for the Chapel Exercises and for public occasions.

Terms.

Piano—With class work in History, Theory and Harmony, $3.00 per month.

Voice—Private work $3.00 per month; class of four in Public School music $1.00; class of eight 50c per month (this course suited to the needs of prospective teachers).

Expression—Private lessons $3.00; class arrangement according to number in class.

DEPARTMENT OF AGRICULTURE.

W. H. Alderman, B. Sc., Director.

This Course in Agriculture offers valuable training to prospective farmers and those preparing for more extensive work in the Agricultural Colleges. It will consist of a treatment of general agriculture in a general way. We will study text books covering the study of soils, manure, commercial fertilizer, rotation of crops, terracing and live-stock. Pupils will be instructed in judging live-stock, handling improved farm implements, spraying trees and plants, and the art of handling the farm like a practical, well-organized machine. The work will be supplemented with bulletins and circulars from experiment stations and from colleges. Students will be required to do practical work assigned by the agriculturalist during the entire course of agriculture. All required work will be graded and must be done promptly and cheerfully.

The Farm._ The farm consists of 62 acres of the upland sandy loam type of soil. The soil being poor in the beginning, small crops are to be expected until we have time to improve it. Our intentions are to improve the soil by growing legumes, by proper terracing and plowing and by the use of barnyard manure. We expect to reduce the expenses of pupils materially by growing peas, beans, potatoes, cane and such other crops as can be used in the boarding department. In addition to these crops, we expect to grow feed stuff for our live stock.

COPIAH-LINCOLN AGRICULTURAL HIGH SCHOOL DORMITORY GIRLS

Extension Work.

It is our desire to be helpful to the farmers of Copiah and Lincoln Counties. There are many problems which we shall be glad to help you solve. We can vaccinate your hogs and cattle against certain diseases; we can stake off your land for corect terracing, which is the most necessary thing towards the conservation of our hill soils; we can spray or show you how to spray your plants to control diseases and insects and in many other ways do things of practical benefit. We hope to be instrumental in organizing various clubs among the boys. Call on us and we shall be glad to help you in any way we can.

Equipment.

The school owns three mules, three cows, two registered Duroc Jersey Hogs, Boarding Department carries its own hogs all the year. The Board of Trustees is planning to secure a number of first class milk cows at an early date. The Farming Department is supplied with wagon, various plows, harrows and small tools. We hope to build a new barn during coming session.

We have just been favored with a splendid Iowa Cream Separator by the Associated Manufacturers' Company, Waterloo, Iowa, to be kept and used by school indefinitely.

MANUAL TRAINING DEPARTMENT.

W. H. Alderman, B. Sc., Instructor.

We are just beginning this very instructive department in our course of study. The first task confronting us will be equipping the department with substantial benches. This work will be done by students under direct supervision of the Manual Training Instructor. The work proper will consist of elementary instruction in wood work, including the use and care of ordinary hand tools, such as planes, squares, saws, chisels, etc. The exercises given and the models executed are designed to make the student familiar with, and give him skill in the use of these tools. Special attention will be given to gluing, scraping, sandpapering, staining, varnishing and rubbing. We shall try to impress the fact upon the pupil that he can take a few tools and make many ornamental and useful things around the house. This course will work well with the new law requiring so much student labor. When we get the proper equipment for this department we heartily believe this will be one of the most fascinating and helpful courses in our school.

ATHLETICS.

This department, while under general supervision of the Superintendent shall be under the direct supervision of Mr. Henry S. Barron. It is our purpose to maintain a high standard of athletics.

Each student who participates in inter-school contests must have a literary standing of not less than seventy-five percent and his deportment must be such that his general average shall be eighty-five per cent.

No profane or obscene language will be tolerated on the field, and those in authority will endeavor to show the students the importance of giving the opponent a square deal.

We are seeking the highest type of athletes, who will ever reflect honor on our school.

Physical development is a necessity. A student may have mental and moral training and be a decided failure in life without health.

It shall be the aim of the school to give ample attention to this department and to cooperate with those taking part but shall expect all athletes to do their full part in all things.

EXAMINATION, GRADATION AND PROMOTION.

Examinations shall be given at the close of first sem-ester and at the close of the second, also, by consent of the Superintendent, during the term as may be found necessary.

Pupils shall be graded on each day's work, and during each month shall be given a written test in each regular topic, which with the average of the daily grade shall make the monthly grade.

The final and passing mark shall be obtained by tak-ing the average of first and second regular examinations and averaging with the average of the monthly grades. To obtain a promotion, pupils must average 70 per cent with not less than 65 per cent on any subject. No exam-ination at the close of either semester shall be considered if below 60 per cent, but a second opportunity for ex-amination shall be offered if desired.

In the monthly column, 1 stands for a perfect work; 2 stands for very satisfactory work; 3 for satisfactory; 4 for unsatisfactory; and 5 for very unsatisfactory; In the examination column, 100 signifies perfect; 95 excel-lent; 85, very good; 70, passable; below 65, a failure.

Deportment, examinations and attendance marked in plain figures.

PHYSICIAN.

Dr. W. L. Little is the school physician and shall attend all cases of illness of boarding students, which shall be free other than medical fee mentioned under Expenses to those in need of such service. He shall promptly attend any accidents that may demand the at-tention of a physician. The school shall provide simple treatment and such drugs as do not demand a prescrip-tion, which shall be dispensed by the Superintendent. All drugs requiring prescriptions shall be paid for by the student, but the prescription shall be issued by the phy-sician free of charge. Every effort will be made to avoid unnecessary prescriptions or drugs not kept in dormitory.

STUDENT LABOR.

We are required by the State Department of Education to exact ten hours of labor each week from all students.

In this work it shall be the aim of the school to teach the best methods of work as well as require first class work. Work shall be graded and no pupil failing in practical work shall be granted a promotion to a higher grade.

The work of boys shall be upon farm in way of general farm work, or upon campus as may be necessary.

Girls of Dormitory shall do general household work, work in poultry yards or buildings as may be assigned.

Should it be found practical students making a high average in literary and practical work may be given privilege for home credits for work upon a certificate by parent and approved by principal and director of Agriculture or Home Science, (form of certificate designed by school).

School and State Department of Education to regulate the number of hours.

Students in the dormitory shall be required to work as may be necessary upon Saturday and **at no time may the student or parent expect permission for the pupil's absence from dormitory on Saturday unless all practical labor has been completed.**

DORMITORY REQUIREMENTS AND REGUALTIONS.

1. Superintendent or Superintendent and Faculty shall make regulations from time to time as may be necessary.

2. Students must furnish for themselves not less than four sheets, quilts as may be needed, towels, soap, shades, water buckets, dippers, pans or wash basins,

combs, brushes, waste buckets, any thing necessary not furnished by school, which consits of bedstead, mattress. wash stand, table, chair, stove, and wardrobe.

Shades must be color No. 41: green, size 8ft.x38in., and secured day of opening or entrance.

3· Students shall keep rooms clean, rights of occupants must be respected by others. Rooms shall be inspected daily, also at unexpected times by unexpected parties, and an accurate grade kept of condition.

4. Students are required to dress neatly but not expensively. An appearance upon campus or especially in school room or dining hall in other than neat dress shall subject student to penalty and if insisted upon to dismissal.

5. **Any lack of personal care of person or of room shall not be tolerated but shall be liable to penalty. Personal effects must in the rooms be placed in proper places.**

6. Meals shall be served at regular hours and pupils must report promptly or forfeit right to the meal.

7. Students must receipt for condition of room and furniture on entrance and shall be held responsible for condition of same. Any damage to furniture or to the building must be paid within one week or pupil dismissed.

8. No pupil shall change room by the consent of any teacher, but must first secure written permission from the Superintendent, which shall show that records have been changed to show rooms vacated and rooms occupied.

9. Privilege of barber work, pressing or tailoring, shoe shining and shoe mending have each been granted to students that they may be done in room in the Administration Building, known as barber shop. Any one infringing upon either of these privileges to have work done in the school by other students or to do work in any room of dormitory or elsewhere shall become subject to immediate dismissal. The room for such shall be open at

stated times to any boy desiring to mend his own shoes or press his own clothes.

GENERAL REGULATIONS.

(All rules and regulations have been accepted by Board of Trustees).

1.   The school buildings and property shall not be used for any public entertainments or shows.

2.   Lectures and affairs of an educational nature may be given only with the consent of the Superintendent.

3.   Recitals and other entertainments given by the School shall be given only with the consent and under the direction of the Superintendent at such times as he may think best.   Other schools or Educational Societies of the two counties desiring to give entertainments must secure consent of Superintendent and pay not less than 50 per cent gross receipts to the School.   Entertainment not provided for schools while giving entertainment.

4.   No advertising matter shall be distributed among the pupils while at school or any article offered for sale upon the grounds, or to pupils upon the grounds.

5.   All teachers boarding shall be subject to dormitory duty and to dormitory regulations.

6.   Any one desiring to see pupil upon the school property shall first state reasons to and receive permission from the Superintendent or teacher who may be in charge.

7.   All teachers and pupils boarding in dormitories shall be required to attend the church and Sunday school of their choice, which shall be stated on entrance.   Sunday night religious services are held at the School and all students of the dormitories required to attend.   Teachers required to attend unless excused in advance.

8.   No games of base-ball, basket-ball, foot-ball, or similar games shall be allowed on Sunday, not even as a practice game.

9. Girls of dormitory shall upon public occasions wear uniforms which shall be made as early as possible after opening of school under direction of Department of Domestic Arts.

10. Girls of dormitory required to do such work in dormitory as may be necessary but usually is not very much for each individual. Each girl required to be provided with white aprons and white caps.

11. **Each pupil must bring plate, cup and saucer, knife, fork and two spoons to be kept in room to be used in case of sickness. Meals not served without them.**

12. No meals served sick ones until ordered by teacher in charge.

13. Parents and guardians requested to visit their children when convenient and no charge for meals while present. The right is reserved to charge others a reasonable rate or to charge those they are visiting if deemed necessary.

14. Those desiring visitors other than father and mother or guardian **first secure consent of superintendent.**

15. At no time shall a gentleman call upon a lady visiting the school or girls of the school nor shall any male student of the school accompany, call upon or attend a lady while visiting school unless by permission of Superintendent at some special social event.

16. No purchases shall be made by any pupil, matron, teacher, or other party than the Superintendent for **tory to go home with another. Permission to go home shall be granted on Saturday morning, students required to remain at school Friday night or forfeit 10% on grades and work extra hours.—Do not ask for exceptions.** said School, nor shall the School be responsible for any claim thus made. Superintendent may delegate this to others by legal provision.

GENERAL RULES FOR PUPILS.

1.   All pupils in the school are required to be regular in attendance, punctual, and pursue a full course of study, to conform to all rules and regulations of the school.

2.   Pupils shall be orderly and neat in care of books, desks, and other property, and shall be held responsible for condition of desk, table or room occupied.

3.   Pupils attending school from home must, if compelled to leave school before the hour of dismissal, bring a written excuse from parent or guardian, and present to Superintendent, otherwise the excuse cannot be granted.

4.   Pupils boarding in dormitories shall be allowed to go home only upon a written request from parent or guardian presented to ·Superintendent. **All practical work must be finished first.** At no time shall a pupil of the dormitories to be allowed to visit in town or community. **Will not give consent for one pupil of dormitory to go home with another.**

5.   Pupils must not

   (a) Come to school after exposure to any infectious disease.

   (b) Pass to a higher grade without taking regular examinations.

   (c) Bring fire arms or fire works of any kind to school.

   (d) Expect to be admitted to school if tardy unless a written excuse is presented on arrival.

6.   Pupils may be suspended for any of the following reasons:

   (a) Deportment falling below the minimum average.

   (b) Violent or pointed opposition to the authority of any teacher in any particular instance.

(c) Conduct or habits which are injurious to others and reflect on the reputation of the school.

(d) When teachers agree that the influence of any pupil is dangerous to those with whom it may come in contact.

(e) Carrying unlawful weapons of any kind.

(f) Persistent indolence and wilful opposition to the general rules of the school.

(g) Any hindrance of trains upon Illinois Central Railroad, boarding of or riding of freight trains or beating way upon passenger trains, any interference with railroad property.

(h) Interfering with electric bells, hydrants, or maliciously meddling with school property.

(i) Leaving school or dormitory without permission of superintendent if in charge, if not of next teacher or party in charge.

(j) Any use of tobacco at school or elsewhere at any time or punished as faculty may see proper.

RULES FOR TEACHERS.

1. Each teacher shall follow a daily program, except by request and consent of the Superintendent, and shall furnish him with detailed information of his department on request.

2. Teachers are held responsible to Superintendent for discipline and deportment of their own rooms, also any campus, hall or dormitory duty to which they may be assigned.

3: Tardiness on the part of a teacher shall not be tolerated.

4. Teachers shall keep such registers and class records, make such reports in writing to the Superintendent daily or at such times as he may require.

5.   Teachers must attend all faculty meetings unless excused by the Superintendent and shall perform such work as may be assigned them. They shall read such school journals and educational books as will aid them in their work and keep them posted with modern ideas of education.

6.   Teachers, whether regular or special, boarding in the dormitory shall perform such duty as may be required during the week or on Saturdays and Sundays.

7.   No teacher shall be entitled to pay for any school month until all reports, records, etc., for that month shall have been made out and approved.

8.   All teachers, whether regular or spcial, must assist the Superintendent in any way requested by him in preparing for commencement or other public meetings and to perform faithfully any assigned duty.

9.   Teachers must cooperate with the Superintendent in all matters pertaining to school work. He is the head of the school and as such is entitled to the cooperation of every teacher, and each shall be expected to comply cheerfully and promptly with any request or rule which he may make.

10.   All teachers shall remain at dormitory at least three week ends ench month.

11.   Lady teachers, regular or special, shall not re-receive calls or accept company of their gentlemen friends during the week at any time except Sunday.

12.   Teachers, male or female, must not give special attention to, receive calls or special attention from pupils.

13.   These rules become a part of the contract of each regular or special teacher and a violation or failure to comply means forfeiture of rights to position.

14.   If compelled to be absent, teachers must be excused by the Superintendent and must pay expense of substitute.

15.   A failure on the part of a teacher to comply with any of the above rules shall be reported by the Superintendent to the Board of Trustees.

ASSISTANT SUPERINTENDENT.

1.   The Assistant Superintendent shall assist the Superintendent in every way possible to promote the general interest of the school.

2.   He shall assume the powers and duties of the Superintendent in his absence.

SUPERINTENDENT.

1.   The Superintendent is the executive officer of the Board of Trustees and shall have general supervision over the school under direction of the Board.

2.   He shall give vigilant attention to the classification of pupils, the character of instruction given, and to the methods of discipline adopted and used.

3.   He shall counsel and direct teachers and render reasonable aid when necessary for the general welfare of the school.

4.   He shall have the general care of the buildings and grounds and shall report to the trustees the needs of the same.

5.   He shall require the teachers to keep a complete record of the attendance and daily standing of each pupil and shall make such reports from time to time to the Trustees as they may request.

6.   It shall be his duty to keep himself and the Board of Trustees informed in regard to the school systems of other leading schools, and other matters as may be of general school interest.

7.   When time will admit, he shall teach such such subjects as he may select, but must not teach such number of topics or classes that duties of supervision be hindered.

8.   He shall hold regular faculty meetings for the purpose of discussing the work and needs of the school with his assistants and to discuss any other educational or professional subjects which will be of value to the teachers, pupils, or school.

9. He shall have power to suspend pupils from school, for cause, subject to the action of the Central Committee of the Board, which shall be considered by them at such time as they may select. It shall also be in his power to reinstate such cases as he may think best without action of the Central Committee.

10. He may make such rules and regulations as may be necessary for the good of the school or any individual.

11. He shall have full cooperation of each teacher, whether regular or special, in the enforcement of any regulations he may make, also the faithful performance of any duty assigned to teachers, and upon failure to receive the same, shall report to the Board of Trustees.

12. He shall keep the financial record of the school and purchase supplies as may be necessary.

ROLL OF STUDENTS—1916-1917.

Preparatory.

Bentz, W. Murl _____Chatawa
Bleecker, Dunk _____Brookhaven
Collins, R. L. _____Wesson
Furr, Addie Nell _____Wesson, R. F. D.
Furr, Wilmer _____Wesson, R. F. D.
Landis, R. J. _____Wesson
Loyd, Clarence _____Wesson, R. F. D.
McDaniels, Harry_____Natalbany, La.
Turnbough, Holton _____Brookhaven

First Year.

Allen, Ethel _____Hazlehurst
Allen, Mary _____Georgetown
Bufkin, Mary _____Wesson, R. F. D.
Bufkin, Henry _____Wesson, R. F. D.
Cannon, Eva Nell _____Wesson
Calcote, Boyd _____Wesson, R. F. D. No. 7
Calcote, Willie _____Wesson, R. F. D. No. 7

Cherry, Colby --Brookhaven
Coleman, Clarence -------------------------Wesson, R. F. D. No. 7
Cox, Hamilton ---------------------------------------Brookhaven
Dampeer, James ---Wesson
Day, Mary ---Wesson
Day, James ---Wesson
Day, Ella ---------------------------------------Wesson, R. F. D.
Dennis, Elvin --Wesson
Furr, Rudolph ---------------------------------------Wesson
Furr, Edith---------------------------------------Wesson, R. F. D.
Ford, Edward --Wesson
Gulley, Tom ---------------------------------------Brookhaven
Harris, William -----------------------------------Hazlehurst
Hartley, Earlie ---Barlow
Hartley, Susie --Allen
Hennington, Pearl ------------------------------------Wesson
Henry, Lucille ----------------------------------Wesson, R. F. D.
Hodges, Modena --Wesson
Kelley, J. B.--Beauregard
Lambert, Effie --Wesson
Lambright, Roy ----------------------------------Wesson, R. F. D.
Lambright, Virgie --------------------------------Wesson, R. F. D.
Lucas, May --------------------------------------Wesson, R. F. D.
Lusk, Bennie ---------------------------------------Beauregard
McRee, Elmer ------------------------------------Union Church
McLaurin, C. G. -------------------------------------Brookhaven
MaGee, Nannie O. -------------------------------------Wesson
May, Birdett -----------------------------------Wesson, R. F. D.
Miller, Helon --------------------------------------McCall Creek
Montgomery, Clyde -----------------------------------Brookhaven
Morgan, Mollie -----------------------------------Wesson, R. F. D.
Mullens, Lessie ---------------------------------------Glancy
Nelson, Sam ------------------------------------Wesson, R. F. D.
Reed, Vernon --------------------------------------Bogue Chitto
Robertson, Lillian -----------------------------------Wesson
Robinson, Annie --Wesson
Sandifer, Mildred ------------------------------------Wesson
Sandifer, Edna --------------------------------------Wesson
Smith, Earlie --------------------------------------Bogue Chitto
Speed, Carrie ----------------------------------Wesson, R. F. D.
Story, William --------------------------------------Beauregard
Sullivan, Will Edna -----------------------------------Carpenter
Thompson, Luther --------------------------------Wesson, R. F. D.
Thurman, Bertha --------------------------------------Wesson
Williams, Walter ------------------------------------Wesson

Second Year.

Alford, James _____Wesson
Allen, Abbie _____Georgetown
Beecham, Dan _____Allen
Bentz, Alvin _____Chattawa
Bondurant, Marguerite _____Wesson
Bowie, Lenie _____Brookhaven
Bufkin, Lona _____Wesson, R. F. D.
Burns, Henry _____Wesson
Byrd, David _____Lucien
Case, Rosa Lee _____Wesson, R. F. D.
Covington, Prentiss _____Wesson, R. F. D.
Davis, Mildred _____Wesson, R. F. D.
Dennis, Inez _____Wesson
Evans, Lawrence _____Wesson, R. F. D.
Fergerson, Florence _____Wesson, R. F. D.
Freeman, Lonie _____Wesson
Furr, Walter _____Wesson, R. F. D.
Furr, Mary _____Wesson
Furr, Gladys _____Allen
Furr, X. L. _____Wesson
Furr, Lillian _____Allen
Graves, Mary Nell _____Wesson
Hall, Mallie _____Glancey
Hartley, M. E. _____Allen
Hoggatt, Son _____Wesson, R. F. D.
Jasper, Mattie Sue _____Carpenter
Keen, Beulah _____Jackson
Lee, Marvin _____Wesson
Lofton, Leonard _____Ollie
Miller, Andy _____Wesson, R. F. D.
Mullen, Mary _____Glancy
Raiford, Ruth _____Wesson, R. F. D.
Raulins, Rhetta _____Bogue Chitto
Rooney, Gertrude _____Wesson
Thurman, Willie Belle _____Wesson
Trim, R. W. _____Conn
Walker, Walter _____Beauregard
White, Lee _____Wesson, R. F. D.
Wilks, Nellie _____Beauregard
Williams, Wilmer _____Wesson
Young, Harvey, _____Carpenter

Junior.

Allen, Nathan _____Brookhaven, R. F. D.
Ashley, Cicero _____Georgetown
Beacham, Nealie _____Wesson, R. F. D.
Britt, Floyd _____Wesson, R. F. D.
Burnaman, Wise _____Brookhaven
Case, Earl _____Wesson, R. F. D.
Claibourn, John, _____Georgetown
Coleman, Sherwood E. _____Carpenter.
Davis, Montie _____Wesson, R. F. D.
Davis, Murray _____Wesson, R. F. D.
Decelle, Louis _____Glancy
Dixon, Myrtle _____Bogue Chitto
Evans, Reginald _____Wesson
Furr, Clyde _____Wesson, R. F. D.
Harrison, Myrtle _____Georgetown
Harrison, Luther _____Georgetown
Harris, Joe _____Hazlehurst
Hennington, Effie _____Wesson
Higdon, Mattie Nell _____Hazlehurst
Leonard, Lola _____Wesson, R. F. D.
Little, Paul _____Wesson
Magee, Bettie _____Wesson
Merwin, Carter _____New Orleans, La.
Middleton, Boyce _____Montgomery
Montgomery, Jeffie _____Wesson, R. F. D.
Montour, Vestelle _____Wesson
Newman, Charles _____Wesson, R. F. D.
*Oliver, Verna _____Wesson
Patterson, Kennedy _____Wesson
Peets, Winnie _____Wesson, R. F. D.
Pope, Ford _____Collins
Porter, Hezekiah _____McCall Creek
Ratcliff, Collie _____Summitt
Slay, May _____Georgetown
Sullivan, Elma _____Carpenter
Thompson, Estelle _____Glancy
Thurman, Cecil _____Crystal Springs
Waldorp, Etta _____Wesson, R. F. D.
Williams, Velma _____Summitt
Williams, Myrtle _____
Youngblood, Myrtle _____Wesson

*Deceased.

Senior.

Ashley, Verd --Georgetown
Beacham, Bettie ---Wesson
Bowie, Melba ---Brookhaven
Douglas, Houston ---Wesson
Durr, Edwin --------------------------------------Brookhaven, R. F. D.
Furr, Fred --Wesson, R. F. D.
Furr, Olian --Wesson
Furr, Luther ---Wesson
Godbold, Levi --Magnolia
Keen, Wesley --Jackson
Keen, Curtis ---Jackson
Lee, Charles --Wesson
Paxton, Fannie --Brookhaven
Price, Ella ---Bogue Chitto
Sandifer, Brilla --Wesson
Sandifer, Anderson --Wesson
Smith, Sam ---------------------------------------Wesson, R. F. D.
Sullivan, Tom ---Meadville
Walker, Emily --Verna
Williams, Dora May --Wesson
Williams, Myrtle --Wesson
Wilson, Roy ---Beauregard

Seniors Graduating—1917.

Ashley, Verd
Beacham, Bettie
Bowie, Melba
Douglass, Houston
Furr, Fred
Keen, Wesley
Keen, Curtis
Lee, Charles

Patterson, Catherine
Price, Ella
Sandifer, Brilla
Sandifer, Anderson
Smith, Sam
Sullivan, Tom
Walker, Emily
Wilson, Roy

Diploma in Music and Expression.
Gladys Furr

Seniors—Graduates 1917.

Cotton, Willis
Furr, Jewell
Little, Ashford
Meathvin, J. H.

Mullican, Holland
Smith, Frank
Weathersby, Minnie

Senior Organization—1917.

Sam Smith, President   Catherine Patterson, Secretary

Lightning Source UK Ltd.
Milton Keynes UK
UKHW050019310119
336364UK00009BA/1773/P